The Art and Soul of African American Interpretation

—— Ywone D. Edwards-Ingram ——

Colonial Williamsburg

The Colonial Williamsburg Foundation
Williamsburg, Virginia

In Memory of Greg James

2025 24 23 22 21 20 19 18 17 16   1 2 3 4 5 6

Library of Congress Cataloging-in-Publication Data

Names: Edwards-Ingram, Ywone, 1961- | Colonial Williamsburg Foundation.
Title: The art and soul of African American interpretation / Ywone
    Edwards-Ingram.
Description: Williamsburg, Virginia : The Colonial Williamsburg Foundation,
    2016. | Includes bibliographical references.
Identifiers: LCCN 2015036564 | ISBN 9780879352806 (hardcover : alk. paper)
Subjects: LCSH: Historic sites--Interpretive
    programs--Virginia--Williamsburg. | African
    Americans--Virginia--Williamsburg--History--18th century. |
    Slavery--Virginia--Williamsburg--History--18th century. | Williamsburg
    (Va.)--History--18th century.
Classification: LCC F234.W7 E35 2016 | DDC 305.896/0730755425209033--dc23 LC record
available at http://lccn.loc.gov/2015036564

Colonial Williamsburg is a registered trade name of The Colonial Williamsburg Foundation,
a not-for-profit educational institution.

The Colonial Williamsburg Foundation
PO Box 1776
Williamsburg, VA 23187-1776
colonialwilliamsburg.org

Printed in the United States of America

Designed by Shanin Glenn

Photography by Tom Green, David M. Doody, Darnell Vennie

Table of Contents

Introduction

Colonial Williamsburg's character interpreters are key to the museum's living history programs. These interpreters, white and black, deepen our understanding of slavery and freedom and of colonial and Revolutionary America.

Interpreting African American characters, enslaved and free, involves particular challenges. This book explores the distinctive nature of that work through the experiences—told in their own words—of six veteran interpreters.

African Americans have played integral roles at the museum since its beginnings in the late 1920s. At first, they were part of a labor force providing services, especially in construction, maintenance, and hospitality. A few also worked as presenters in the Historic Area's kitchens, exhibition buildings, and trade shops. Several African American men worked with the carriage-ride program in the 1940s. Some were coachmen-interpreters who took guests, including dignitaries, around the Historic Area. Colonial Williamsburg's film *The Story of a Patriot* (1956) included African Americans, and *Music of Williamsburg* (1960) featured African American musicians.

It was not until 1979 that Colonial Williamsburg introduced
living history interpreters, including African Americans. As
costumed interpreters, African Americans played enslaved as
well as free blacks who had lived in Williamsburg during and a
little time after the Revolution. During the 1980s a handful of
vignettes and street plays featuring costumed African American interpreters in various roles evolved into an organized
program about African American history and slavery.

During the early years of this programming, the majority
of Colonial Williamsburg's guests saw live interpretations of

slavery for the first time. Many of them did not know how to react. Rex Ellis, who helped to pioneer these presentations on slavery and freedom, recalled how revolutionary these programs were at the time. They presented information about the harsh realities of slave life and explored topics like racism and brutality. The work was emotionally and intellectually demanding, and the interpreters had to encourage themselves and each other and come to grips with their own views about slavery. And they had to deal with a range of receptions, positive and negative.

By the late 1980s, Colonial Williamsburg presented a wide array of interpretative programs. A music program featured African and African American music, including activities like responsive renditions of songs, playing of instruments, storytelling, and dance performances. There were tours and educational outreach activities as well.

Colonial Williamsburg also increased and diversified its research and applied the results to what people saw in the Historic Area. It modified interiors of buildings to show more living and working spaces for slaves and invested in changing its landscape settings to include reconstructed slave quarters and more auxiliary buildings. A slave quarter was built at Carter's Grove plantation, which was later replaced by more accessible sites, including Great Hopes Plantation.

Ellis remembered one challenge (and opportunity) that arose at Carter's Grove. Many guests skipped the slave quarter and headed directly to the mansion. To do so, they had to cross a pedestrian bridge.

> Arthur Johnson was interpreting at the site. He stood at the end of the bridge. The visitors would stop short of the exit from the bridge to hear what was on his mind. "I know you are heading on up to the mansion," he would tell them, "but before you go, let me ask you a question: Is anyone here related to the Burwells, the colonial owners of Carter's Grove . . . anyone at all?" When he received a "no" to this question, he then pointed to the slave quarter and said, "Welcome home."

Guests got the point that the houses of middling and poor white people were a lot more similar to those of slaves than to the mansion. Ellis said Johnson "brought history up close, relevant, and personal in a way I'm sure few who were blessed enough to have Arthur as their interpreter would soon forget."

In the 1990s, Colonial Williamsburg added more interpretive scenes between whites and blacks and many presentations of disquieting topics, some with audience participation. In 1994, under the direction of Christy Coleman, Colonial Williams-burg staged a single-day event of an estate sale that included

▲ A simulated slave auction challenged Colonial Williamsburg interpreters . . . and guests.

a reenacted slave auction. News of the plan for the auction provoked a range of emotions, including anger and anguish. Coleman knew that this was a very sensitive topic, but she was also well aware of its potential to inform about the horrors of slavery. She believed it was the right time to present the auction, and she herself portrayed an enslaved person placed on the block. After the event, many people expressed relief, and some who had objected to the idea applauded Colonial Williamsburg for the sensitive way it dealt with the topic.

Over the years, Colonial Williamsburg has broadened its programs to establish and maintain a more holistic interpre-

▲ Panel members on the set for a televised program on the slave trade

tation of the colonial and Revolutionary eras including all the peoples involved in that history. Its Revolutionary City programs let guests interact with a diverse group of historical characters who lived in or visited Williamsburg around the time of the American Revolution. Electronic media and Internet programs, blog posts, games, podcasts, and exhibits have all brought history into the digital age.

Amidst myriad practices of interpretation, Colonial Williamsburg's historical interpreters remain the key to the success of its living history programs. For African American interpreters, the work presents special challenges. Their heritage—their own connections to enslaved and free Africans and their descendants in the Americas—informs and also complicates their work.

What motivates these interpreters? What challenges do they face and how do they deal with them? How do they find and use teachable moments?

This book records the reflections of six of Colonial Williamsburg's veteran interpreters: James Ingram Jr., Emily James, Hope Wright, Arthur Johnson, Rosemarie McAphee, and Gregory James. Two of the interpreters, James Ingram and Emily James, base their characters on historical figures of great influence—Gowan Pamphlet, an enslaved man who pastored an early black Baptist church, and Edith Cumbo, a free black woman who was counted in a 1782 census as head of a household in Williamsburg. Ingram and James are part of a select group of Colonial Williamsburg interpreters designated "nation builders" that also includes Thomas Jefferson, George Washington, and Patrick Henry.

What goes into creating characters like Pamphlet and Cumbo, or the enslaved tavern man named Wil, or the enslaved domestic woman named Eve? Throughout this book, the interpreters discuss the research process, training, and skills that undergird and inform the presentations of eighteenth-century characters and the teaching of history. They explain how they weave together details of life from different types of research including working with limited historical documentation about some of the colonial characters they portray. The interpreters show how they model styles of behavior and use a variety of techniques like storytelling and dialogue to enrich their accounts of the past. They tell of the connections they have made between past and present, some planned and some unanticipated. Their insights are invaluable to all who care about living history.

James Ingram Jr.

 JAMES INGRAM JR. started his career at Colonial Williamsburg in the mid-1990s with a long history of serving as a leader in Christian ministry. He continues to be a source of inspiration through his engaging and powerful interpretations on history and religion. Over the years, he has taught and presented a wide range of programming to help various audiences, including participants in interpreter and teacher training programs, to have a better understanding of eighteenth-century Williamsburg and slavery.

Ingram has portrayed more than twenty-five historical characters, not only for Colonial Williamsburg but also for programs at other museums, academic conferences, churches, schools, and historical sites. His popularity and talents have been showcased in multimedia products including the 2006 Emmy award–winning education film produced by Colonial Williamsburg *No Master Over Me.*

Ingram's own theological training and experience have helped him to develop his methodologies for researching and interpreting his main portrayal for Colonial Williamsburg: that of the life and ministry of Baptist pastor Gowan Pamphlet. Since 1998, he has been portraying Pamphlet, who was probably one of the earliest ordained black preachers in America.

Gowan Pamphlet

Gowan Pamphlet paved a pathway of recognition for his Christian ministry centered on a gospel of equality. Between the 1770s and 1790s, Pamphlet built a ministry and sustained a congregation that numbered five hundred people in 1791. Oral tradition suggests that Pamphlet's earliest meetings were clandestine ones in brush arbors or overgrowth at Green Spring plantation in the 1770s, several miles south of Williamsburg. By 1781, the congregation consisted of about two hundred people. It was probably around that time that the group began meeting closer to Williamsburg on land called Racoon Chase, south of the College of William and Mary.

Pamphlet's accomplishments are remarkable in light of his status as an enslaved man for about forty years. His legal owner Jane Vobe was the proprietor of the King's Arms Tavern on the main street of Williamsburg. Pamphlet became a free man when Vobe's son, David Miller, manumitted him in 1793.

James Ingram is himself a preacher and compares his Christian fellowship
with that of Gowan Pamphlet.

Of the many roles that I've played over the years, Gowan Pamphlet
is definitely my number one favorite because of a lot of similarities we
have. I'm not saying that interpreters take on the spirit of a person from
the past, but sometimes life presents you with an opportunity that you
never ever thought would come your way. And this was the case when I
was presented with the role of Gowan.

Here's a prime example of why I relate so well to Gowan: Gowan
Pamphlet applied to join the Dover Baptist Association of Virginia in
1791. He applied for his church of over five hundred members to be part
of this association. The Dover Association was the only association of
Baptists that made a statement about abolition. I am sure that's what
drew Gowan to that association. When I finished seminary in 1988, before I knew anything about Gowan, the first Baptist association I joined

The following is a transcription of Pamphlet's deed of manumission:

Know all men by these presents that I David Miller of York County do hereby
manumit emancipate and set free a Negro man named and called Gowin
Pamphet, and I do for myself my Heirs
executors and administrators hereby
declare the said Negro man Gowin Pamphet
exonerated of and from all services
whatsoever and do hereby declare him to
be a free man, and I do renounce all Right
title Interest claim and demand whatsoever
to the said Slave. In Witness whereof I have
hereunto set my Hand and affixed my seal
this twenty fifth day of September 1793.

^ Gowan Pamphlet's deed of manumission

was the Dover Baptist Association. I can actually remember being at a convention where the speaker said, "We are one of the most historical associations in the history of America as far as the Baptists are concerned in Virginia." I almost feel like I am continuing Gowan's legacy. He was among the earliest black preachers to join the Dover Association, and it was the same one I joined when I finished my seminary.

Ingram sees many similarities between preaching and interpreting.

Preaching is a natural training ground for this kind of interpretation. Not only in terms of speaking in front of lots of people, but also you have to care about people and be patient about giving them information. You have to be a teacher but also a sort of repository of information, including taboos, things you don't talk about in society.

Gowan Pamphlet

It was also in 1793 that the prominent Dover Baptist Association of Virginia accepted his church's application for membership. Pamphlet attended the association's annual meeting in October 1793 and participated in other annual meetings of the Dover Association. The minutes of the 1793 meeting included this item: "The Baptist church of black people at Williamsburg, agreeably to their request, was received into this Association, as they could not have done better in their circumstances than they have."

As a free black, Pamphlet had the right to own land. By 1805, he had acquired a quarter of a lot in the city and fourteen acres of land in James City County. Pamphlet also owned a horse, perhaps for his travels to reach congregants in various locations in and near Williamsburg. He served as pastor of his church until his death around 1807. The present-day congregation of this historic church meets in a modern-day structure near Colonial Williamsburg's Historic Area.

When I grew up, in my house we didn't talk about slavery, we didn't talk much about religion, although we went to church on Sundays, and we didn't talk much about politics, and now I'm doing all three. These "taboo" subjects that you don't talk about if you want to have good friends—now I talk about all these subjects daily as Gowan.

Like preaching, interpreting is a mission. I don't want people imagining me as a crackpot, but it's almost a calling. This information that we have to give people is so vital for their own understanding of whence they came and who they are in society that you feel like you have been placed with Colonial Williamsburg to do this. If you listen to the stories of why people come to interpret with Colonial Williamsburg, they didn't ever think they would be here. They happened to end up here or got transfixed while visiting here and then were caught up in the whole story of what we teach. They feel like they really have to give it to the people.

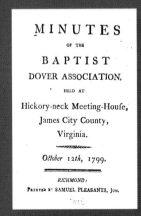

MINUTES
OF THE
BAPTIST
DOVER ASSOCIATION,
HELD AT
Hickory-neck Meeting-House,
James City County,
Virginia.
October 12th, 1799.
RICHMOND:
PRINTED BY SAMUEL PLEASANTS, JUN.

11. *Hickory-neck*, John Goodall, Wm. Goodail, John Goodall, jr. Hendley Taylor.
12. *Upper College*, John Gary, James Gary.
13. *Hanover*, Jesse Davis, Thomas White.
14. *Chickahominy*, John Winn,* Jas. Cawthon,* Jesse Payne.*
15. *Tuckaho*,
16. *Gloucester*, William Leigh, Francis Leigh.
17. *Glebe Landing*, John Clarke, William Simco.
18. *Williamsburg*, Gowin Pamphlet, Israel Camp.
19. *Hermitage*, John Healy, John Jesse, James Healy.
20. *Dover*, William Webber.

^ Minutes of the Baptist Dover Association

What if someone, on hearing a sermon, becomes converted and wants to be baptized?

One of our interpreters actually asked this question of Dr. John Turner, who was manager of religious studies and programs, when he was leading a training session: "Your preacher boys are out there preaching for real. And what would happen if one of the guests becomes converted?" His reply was that he was very aware of what we were teaching and preaching in our interpretation, and, if one of the guests falls into a state of conversion, then that person would need to find a church in his or her community. So if this was happening in my presentation, I would direct the guest to the particular denomination of choice for more counseling and guidance. I am not surprised when these things happen—and guests have shared this with me in private conversations—for I don't curtail my sermons. These are real prayers, these are real Bible verses, for all these are parts of the character's history.

Ingram embraces new information from continued research, validates it, and folds it into his character interpretation.

Gowan Pamphlet has been portrayed in Williamsburg since 1979. But the character Rex Ellis created then is nowhere near the Gowan that I have created. Back then, there were literally just a few paragraphs about Gowan, written by Linda Rowe, one of Colonial Williamsburg's historians. But she has since found more information, enough to write and publish articles about him. Now, more researchers are including him in their writings. For example, Jan Couperthwaite, who volunteers in our library, is doing groundbreaking research on dissenting New Light preachers in colonial Virginia and has found additional details about Gowan.

At times, I've had to say, "Well, I'm really not sure about that, but let me ask other folks." Any audience I've been with has appreciated that. They know you're not going to make up something just to make them think that you are so knowledgeable. We don't know every single thing. I learn every single day. I know that is hard for people to understand. Sometimes I've had to redo my interpretation because some new information has come out. I used to say for years, when we talked about slave laws and especially in the colony of South Carolina, that it was illegal for slaves to read or write. Recently, evidence has come out that it was not illegal for them to read, only for them to write. Now you feel really bad because you've told thousands and thousands of people misinformation. You didn't do it because you wanted to give them misinformation, but that was the information you had. Don't be afraid to say that "as far as I know" this is the way, and be ready to change your information.

The word in most historical museums, or anywhere else for that matter, is that we just don't have the information on slavery. That is now, I hope, starting to dissolve because now we realize the methodologies for

researching enslaved people. Over the years, we have added more and more information. We had a breakthrough about Gowan about five years ago.

We know more about oral traditions, stories that are passed on through generations. We also realized that, if we study the people that Gowan was around, maybe somewhere down the line someone had written something about Gowan—and that is exactly what happened. We found medical records from Dr. Galt and Dr. Barraud in their accounts with Mrs. Vobe and her son, David Miller. They show medical treatment for their enslaved man Gowan.

Before the Revolution, Baptists and other dissenters from the Church of England—black or white, bonded or free—could not legally preach because they refused to be licensed by the General Court in

Williamsburg. Add to that the general fear of religious gatherings of slaves as fomenting rebellion, and it was necessary for them to gather in wooded areas for protection against discovery by slave patrols. Based on oral tradition, we understand that by 1776 Gowan's congregation had started out at Green Spring plantation, a few miles from Williamsburg. Records show that the group had two hundred members in 1781 and had moved to a secluded area known as Racoon Chase on the outskirts of Williamsburg. It was in Racoon Chase that Jesse Cole, also according to oral tradition, was hunting when he heard melodious hymn singing coming from this area that bordered his land. As land records show, at least by 1804 Cole owned property on Nassau Street not far from the Public Hospital. He was moved to turn over his carriage house on Nassau Street to the congregation for a makeshift meeting place. In 1856 the old carriage house was replaced with a handsome brick church building that served the congregation for another one hundred years.

Gowan Pamphlet is featured, along with George and Martha Washington, Patrick Henry, and Thomas Jefferson, in Colonial Williamsburg's programs about "nation builders."

Gowan sort of broke the glass ceiling. The foundation can take a bow for initiating a program of nation builders instead of just founding fathers. This is far more inclusive.

We are like movie stars. We sign autographs, we have our pictures taken, and we're in the *Revolutionary City* book. Guests don't want James Ingram's autograph—they want Gowan Pamphlet's. At the Visitor Center, before you go in to see the introductory film *The Story of a Patriot,* you might see a big poster of me saying that I will be speaking at the St. George Tucker House in the Historic Area. As a nation builder interpreter,

I am no longer playing many other characters because I could run into a credibility issue if people saw me as someone else.

Over the years, I became a strong interpreter. This comes through a lot of hard work, a lot of dedication, a lot of time invested, and years of experience. I became a mentor for other interpreters, so I have to carry myself in a certain manner. Because I am a mentor and also a veteran interpreter, other interpreters are always watching, so I have to be a leader. I think it takes five years before interpreters reach the point where they feel comfortable fielding questions from audiences.

I am given assignments off-site and out of state, too. I am an ambassador for Colonial Williamsburg.

In portraying Pamphlet, Ingram focuses on his role as an enslaved person. But, his role also sheds light on other aspects of the period, especially politics and racial relations, and of course religion.

What really attracted me to Colonial Williamsburg was the focus on slavery. I was born in Virginia, and the first six years of my schooling I came to Williamsburg, Jamestown, and Yorktown on elementary school field trips, but I never saw African American interpreters and I never thought about programs on slavery. I do remember some coachmen that were black but didn't consider Colonial Williamsburg's Historic Area as a place where you could hear about the story of slavery or the history of African Americans.

In eighteenth-century Williamsburg, you couldn't get away from slavery because you were in a slave society. But there were free people who were always affecting you, so, as a character interpreter, you have to talk about them. For instance, Gowan was in the King's Arms Tavern. He was a slave there. But who were the people coming into the tavern and part of Gowan's world? Men like George Washington, Thomas Jefferson, James Madison, and George Mason.

As Pamphlet might have put it, "George Washington has slaves, so when he comes into the tavern, I talk to his right-hand man, who is Billy Lee, a slave. I know what is going on at Mount Vernon through my conversations with Lee; I know what is going on at Monticello from my conversations with Jupiter. All the right-hand men of these men are Negroes, so I know a lot about what is going on at their plantations."

Like other African American interpreters, Ingram has heard criticisms both from those who feel interpreters portray slavery too harshly and from those who feel they whitewash history.

Slavery was a complex institution. This is a complex story. Many people come to Colonial Williamsburg's Historic Area with preconceived ideas about "how it was back then." Here you are, Joe or Jill interpreter, and you've now all of a sudden just shattered everything that

they thought about the institution of slavery. For some, their conception is like in the movie *Gone with the Wind,* and you're talking about punishment, brutality, selling people away from husband, wife, children, father, mother, aunt, uncle. You start talking to guests, and you are going to drive some of them to tears. Sometimes they don't want to look at you. Not everyone is suited, not everyone can do this, because you're going to get emotionally caught up in some of the things that you're going to be talking about. This is a bloody story.

If you have more black people in your audience, you might just go into that punishment a little bit deeper, you might go into that law that was written down. You will give them a little extra because you know that, even if they don't have the academic background, they know if you are sugarcoating or dancing around certain topics. And you are going to have people, especially African Americans, who will accuse you of not talking about the horror, not talking about the blood, not talking about the lashes—of sugarcoating the history.

What they don't understand, what we are telling them, is that each household would have been different, each individual owner different, each individual slave person different. Everyone did not face being lashed every single day, but still you were in an institution of legal slavery, and that means that you would be a slave for the rest of your life. People need to take away that the problem with this institution of slavery *was the law.*

You have to be patient; that is one particular skill you have to bring to this job. The guest is not necessarily right. This is a learning institution, and sometimes education can lead to friction.

Ingram changes his emphasis for different audiences.

I've had Sandra Day O'Connor in my audience behind the Coffeehouse. I didn't know she was there until I saw some people with little things in their ears walking around. I turned around, and Sandra Day O'Connor and all her grandchildren and her children were sitting right there. She's a retired U.S. Supreme Court justice, so all of a sudden the law became very important to my interpretation.

If I have a group that includes children, I always make them part of what I'm doing. I make them realize how important they are. I broaden the interpretation to let them know that children, including slave children and indentured children, were part of the society. I tell them that they are part of these stories that we are talking about and that they are important because the children are the future. I tell them I am not going to be here always, I am going to be gone on with the ancestors, but you are going to be responsible for ruling the country.

If I have a group of children, then my language is going to change, my whole demeanor is going to change. I am going to be more interactive with the children because you want them to kind of play. But I don't think you can do a whole program dancing and shucking and jiving. I always have to think about my credibility, especially as a nation builder.

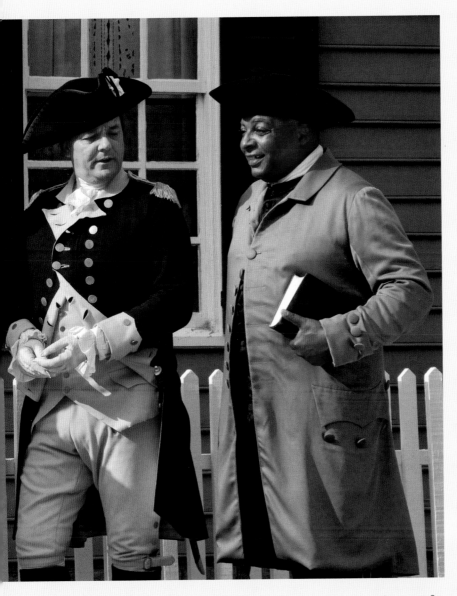

Regardless of the audience, it's crucial that an interpreter stays in character for first-person interpretations.

I use the language of the period, in this case the eighteenth century. And you don't want to bring in modernisms because people then won't get on board—you don't want to talk about Pepsi-Cola and Coca-Cola and Lay's potato chips and all the other stuff of life in the twenty-first century. Modern expressions and slang are out as well. There are other ways to relate. You can talk about sarsaparilla and small beer. You have to watch what you wear and carry. No cell phone in your pocket or Nike tennis shoes beneath your eighteenth-century garb.

I don't have to come out of character to teach a twenty-first-century person what I need them to know. I can just tell by the way someone interacts with me that I must be hitting topics that person is dealing with on a daily basis. There are commonalities that, no matter what century you are talking about, most people experience each day. You have to have the discipline to stay in the historic period that you are in yet still teach about things that people are dealing with in the twenty-first century.

What about live broadcasts for educational programs?

It is a special opportunity to reach children. They get a chance to ask questions about history in their own way. Usually, their questions are based on what they have seen in the historical scenes Colonial Williamsburg has produced. More than likely, I am part of the panel answering questions if I am in the production, so it gives me a chance to explain what I've done as accurately as possible. It is a good way to teach about the past, using the studio and the classroom.

Do kids' questions ever surprise Ingram?

Always! Children ask questions innocently, so they ask better questions. If we're going to get stumped or shocked, it is usually by a question from a child.

Ingram is always on the lookout for more information about history.

I spend much time researching and reading almost anything I get my hands on to give me more information to broaden my interpretation, to make my interpretation clearer. The gathering of information is like a journey. The reward of the journey is finding the right information, so, when you give the information, people will know that it is thoroughly researched and it is highly credible. You have to be credible; you can't just make things up. Your interpretation should be based on good research whether you do it yourself or access the information from historians, architectural specialists, archaeologists, and other researchers. Research is the primary tool. And you have to use it to build your skills and increase your confidence.

Emily James

EMILY JAMES has a knack for putting her audience at ease and establishing a familiarity with them. She has over twenty-seven years of experience representing different people of the past and playing key roles in a range of interpretive programs.

James has interpreted roles as a personal servant, a cook, and a folk healer among others, drawing on information from historical documents about individuals of the eighteenth century. James serves as a mentor for other interpreters and helps in planning and introducing new programs. Individuals from many schools and colleges, church groups, family groups, and civic organizations have benefited from her interpretations.

Nowadays, you can find her portraying a free black woman named Edith Cumbo. Cumbo is among the cast of eighteenth-century characters Colonial Williamsburg calls "nation builders." James presents

Cumbo as someone who interacts well with both whites and blacks in Williamsburg. Cumbo made a living in a slave society defined by laws and practices of racial discrimination. James's presentations imply much about Cumbo's family and about the particularities of living as a free person when most other African Americans in the town were held in bondage. Cumbo was the head of a household but with far more limited rights than white women.

Edith Cumbo

Edith Cumbo was a free African American woman who lived in Williamsburg during and after the American Revolution. Like other free blacks, she had limited rights and privileges but could own land and slaves and could choose her own work and keep her earnings. Cumbo also had rights in court and could use the laws of Virginia to adjudicate wrongs done to her property and person. Free blacks generally maintained close ties with their relatives and friends, who provided supportive networks in a society where the majority of blacks were enslaved, and Cumbo was probably no exception.

Cumbo's freedom was not a gift, nor did she earn or buy it. Her status was conferred to her at birth following a Virginia law passed in the seventeenth century. The law

James prepares to interpret Cumbo by assuming characteristics that made it possible for a free black woman to live and work in Williamsburg in the last quarter of the eighteenth century.

First, I clear my mind to become that person and wear that person's shoes. You have to connect to the time period that you are interpreting. History is about connecting the past with the present. Interpreters are the mediators and the funnel that directs that flow and makes it understandable. As an interpreter, my goal is to show how the past is applicable to people's lives today.

assigned enslaved or free status to a child based on whether the mother was a slave or a free person.

> Seventeenth-century law about the status of children in Virginia

170   LAWS OF VIRGINIA,

                                                    ACT XII.

Edit., 1733 and   *Negro womens children to serve according to the condi-*
1752.   *tion of the mother. (a)*

Parvis 111.   **WHEREAS** some doubts have arrisen whether
Children to be   children got by any Englishman upon a negro woman
bond or free,   should be slave or ffree, *Be it therefore enacted and de-*
according to   *clared by this present grand assembly,* that all children
the condit'n of   borne in this country shalbe held bond or free only ac-
their mother.   cording to the condition of the mother, *And* that if
Double fines   any christian shall committ ffornication with a negro
for fornication   man or woman, hee or shee soe offending shall pay
with a negro.   double the fiues imposed by the former act.

I believe that I have a psychological connection to Edith Cumbo. When I read her story and learn of the strength of her character, I compare her character traits with mine. They just blend together; it's like having compatible DNA. We connect.

You have to tool and retool yourself when you are an interpreter. I read historical documents and books, and I talk to experts. These are essential parts of the research process. Different experts say different things, but you have to find your own historical clarity by weighing the evidence.

It takes time to become a skilled interpreter.

I believe that the very least amount of time to get to a high level is about five years. The best way to understand this process is to compare it with that of a child's educational development from kindergarten to the teen years. Then comes a time for competency and maturity.

Now, if an interpreter is not improving in his or her roles, that's a performance issue between management and the interpreter. But it is also a matter that can be helped with training. When I was a supervisor

Edith Cumbo

In a census record of 1782, Cumbo is listed as head of a household with two other people living with her; they may or may not have been relatives. Exercising her limited rights, Cumbo filed a lawsuit in York County in June 1778 suing Adam White for trespass, assault, and battery. It appears that this case was dismissed because the parties involved did not attend the court hearing.

Although her work skills and occupation are unknown, Cumbo, like many African American females in the town, probably worked as a domestic laborer, likely a laundress or a seamstress, for white households. But unlike the vast number of enslaved domestics, Cumbo would have received payment for her work and perhaps, of interpreters, I created a monologue for an interpreter that covered the specific interpretive points that I felt he needed to address to accomplish his task. I also coached him on body language and voice inflection. But people still need to develop their own skills and be capable to work on their own. Working with your interpretation and making sure that it is improving is like going through a life passage; it's like a fruit coming to maturity after a while.

especially important for someone of African ancestry during that period, she had the right to choose her employers.

Cumbo may have attended Gowan Pamphlet's church in Williamsburg, though any affiliation Cumbo had with this group would not have precluded her attendance at the established Bruton Parish Church.

^ Record of Cumbo's lawsuit against Adam White for assault and battery

James takes pride in talking about slavery.

I get the privilege to tell the story of my ancestors to a modern-day audience—not only of their sufferings but of their contributions to the making of America. When I do my interpretation, I feel the strength of their African blood flowing in my veins. When they were forced onto slave ships from the port of Guinea and various other slave ports in Africa, they didn't give up. If they had given up, if the majority had committed suicide, peoples of African ancestry in America and other parts of the world would have been extinct.

Am I ashamed of my costume? A big no! It is part of the package. To be ashamed of your ancestors would mean that you're ashamed of who you are as a descendant of Africans. I am proud to be black. If you're not accepting who you are, this shows a lack of self-confidence. You have to look at the costume you wear as how society was at the time, and as the society changed, the fashion changed, too. When we wear costumes, there is no need to be ashamed; we are representing the eighteenth century. That's what you signed up for when you took this job.

What about topics suitable for mature audiences only?

My task is to tell about the history and to answer guests' questions. Once I know the answer, I will professionally answer the question. If and when necessary, I take them aside and explain things that I can't say in front of everyone. You have to know your audience, for example, if children are there. If I cannot answer a question, I direct them to someone who I know has the answer. Sometimes, the guests want to know how procreation happened, I mean how a couple managed to engage in these acts when there was no privacy, especially when many people, including children, lived in the same quarter. I tell them couples found private places and created situations that would cause them to be alone together, like going off to the stable or sending the children away on some errands.

Enslaved people were wise, and they knew how to deal with certain conversations and private acts in crowded living conditions. I dealt with these mature questions from guests when I did my interpretation at Wetherburn's Tavern many years ago. I talked in a whisper to people who were in proximity. Also I directed other family members to take the children to nearby venues.

James also has the skills to interpret to groups from diverse backgrounds.

I interpret to special groups like foreigners and donors. The foundation trusts me to do such groups and to be in programs all over the United States. I have been asked, by special requests, to do programs for families with adopted children from diverse backgrounds, such as mixed-race families. These usually are white families who adopted black children and want them to know about their own African American history.

I like using my presentations of Edith Cumbo to address family types and relationships. My coworkers and managers know that I have experience in this area. They trust me to perform my duties in a professional manner. I have been working at it for twenty-seven years and have learned much about interpretation and about people. You have to be balanced. White kids need to know the history, too. I tell them that Edith's mother was white, and this allowed her daughter to have certain rights in the society that some blacks did not have, especially the ones who were slaves. Edith worked and conducted business in a town where the population was almost equally divided between whites and blacks.

James speaks frankly to guests about slavery.

When I am sitting in the parlor at the St. George Tucker House, my character Edith Cumbo tells her guests, "St. George and his wife, Mistress Lelia, would not have me sitting in this armchair, but what they don't know will not hurt them. You all can keep a quiet tongue in your head? Because my mama always said, 'You do not tell all you see or tell all you know.'" I provocatively pull the guests into Edith's world, and then they know that they can ask me any questions.

I use Edith Cumbo's story to focus on the 52 percent of Williamsburg's population that were in bondage around the time of the American Revolution. I say, "You don't see them around here because they are behind where the masters are living. They are in the courtyards. They use spaces above the kitchens, laundries, and stables as sleeping areas. Most of their living is outdoor toiling, and they are busy because they are in bondage."

I talk about my own brothers who served in the Revolutionary War. I talk about the plights and conditions of camp life during the winter and the reasons why blacks are fighting in the army although they are not considered equal. But they are serving their country because this is their home.

James also speaks directly about women's issues.

I talk about the limited rights of all women in the eighteenth century. I explain that they were not just dependents. Some of them even owned land and managed their own households. I want the guest to know about the lives of single mothers and unmarried women. I use

Thomas Jefferson's Declaration of Independence to talk about areas pertaining to women and the plight of the sons and daughters of Africa.

Although Edith is a free woman, and freedom is a blessing from the Almighty God, she has seen many things and knows what slavery had done to black people.

Hope Wright

 Hope Wright practically grew up with living history. She started working for Colonial Williamsburg as a junior interpreter. She has participated in many on- and off-site programs and media productions.

Wright regularly plays the role of a "contextualist," which is similar to a modern moderator, for programs about enslaved and free blacks in eighteenth-century Williamsburg. She introduces these programs, tells the audience what to expect, and guides them on how to participate and how to interact with the interpreters.

Wright, however, is better known for her role as Eve, an enslaved person in the household of Peyton Randolph and his wife, Betty Randolph. Wright plays her role with dignity and grace. She portrays the delicate balance that a personal maidservant had to maintain in a household of an important official of the city.

Eve

Eve was an enslaved woman in the household of Peyton and Elizabeth (Betty) Randolph. Peyton Randolph was Speaker of the House of Burgesses in Williamsburg from 1766 until 1775 and elected as the first president of the Continental Congress in 1774. The Randolphs had many enslaved people living on a property with a substantial residence and many auxiliary buildings in the town's core: the place was more like an urban plantation.

Peyton Randolph died in October 1775, and an inventory of his estate dated January 5, 1776, lists Eve along with twenty-six other slaves and shows that Eve was one of five slaves valued at one hundred British pounds. This high valuation suggests that she was very skilled. Eve was probably the personal maid of Betty Randolph, which probably explains her mistress's focus on her activities. The widow Randolph became Eve's legal owner after Peyton died.

What is a contextualist? How does a contextualist enhance the guest experience?

A contextualist informs the audience about the settings of the program, giving information about the time period and the place where the event is taking place, and especially who they are going to meet. It is important that a contextualist does not give away too much information about the program but rather briefs the audience on what to expect.

I include historical facts in my introduction. For example, when I introduce "Daniel's Dilemma," a program that takes place at Great Hopes Plantation, I put everything in context, but it is short, five minutes. The program is about an enslaved foreman whose job responsibilities, at times, conflict with his ties to other enslaved people. I talk about agriculture, and I point out the main tasks involved in tobacco production. It is a good program even without this introduction, but this overview puts the guests in a different mindset. I am not directing them on what to think but only suggesting. I also reinforce rules about taking photographs and using cell

In 1780, Betty Randolph bequeathed both Eve and George, Eve's son, to her niece Ann Copeland. In 1781, Eve escaped the Randolph household with fifteen-year-old George. (George was probably born in 1766 since he was baptized on July 6, 1766, at Bruton Parish Church.)

^ Peyton Randolph inventory

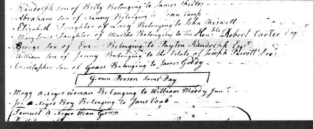
^ Bruton Parish Register

phones, but I do so playfully. I would say, "We are going back in the past. We do not need cell phones and cameras for the eighteenth century."

As the contextualist, my role is to cover the entrance and the exit of a program. I can share historical information during these times. Normally, I don't get questions when I am introducing a program, but after the program I introduce the performers as twenty-first-century persons

Eve

In February 1782, Betty Randolph's nephew Harrison Randolph advertised for Eve's return.

> TWENTY DOLLARS REWARD,
>
> FOR apprehending EVE, a Negro woman flave, who left York after the furrender; fhe is about forty years old, very black and flender, has a fmall mouth for a Negro, and a remarkable mole on her nofe: She has fince been feen on her way to Hampton. She carried with her a variety of ftriped and checked Virginia cloth cloathes. Whoever delivers her to the fubfcriber in Richmond, fhall receive the above reward.
>
> HARRISON RANDOLPH.

^ *Virginia Gazette* advertisement

and their characters. Usually, the guests choose to address the characters in the eighteenth century.

Wright is interested in exploring connections between women's history and black history.

A black woman's story is a powerful way to show women's roles and contributions. You have to look at the individual story; each story is unique. Both during and after slavery, black women worked from a position of hidden strength, helping to provide for their own households as well as those of whites. They had various duties and worked in many spheres, including taking care of children, black as well as white.

Society viewed women as dependent, and black women had a double bondage. Unlike white women, who were usually part of a single household, many black women were part of both black households and white households at the same time. However, some situations were

In July 1782, Betty Randolph added a codicil to her will noting that she had sold Eve:

> Whereas Eve's bad behaviour laid me under the necessity of selling her, I Order and direct the money she sold for may be laid out in purchasing two Negroes Viz. a Boy & girl, the Girl I give to my Niece Ann Coapland in lieu of Eve, in the same manner that I had given Eve. The Boy I give to Peyton Harrison—Son of my Brother Carter Harrison, to him & his heirs forever.

^ Codicil to Betty Randolph's will

great equalizers, such as life-cycle events and life changes like childbirth and illnesses. Black women and white women came together to work through and deal with these situations.

Wright bases her interpretation of Eve on her own research and presents her as a confident person with a strong personality.

I present Eve as a person who was not downtrodden. Her speech would have been polished. She had been accustomed to the life of the gentry since she lived in that type of household. But I believe she would switch her behavior. Her behavior would have been different when she was among her own kin and community. Eve would have been well aware of her place, and she would have remembered her social and legal status as an enslaved person.

I do research on enslaved women. I bring primary sources to bear on my interpretation. I look at runaway advertisements, for example. I bring the experience of a black woman, and this informs my understanding of black women's history. I can draw connections to what is happening in the black community today.

I try to focus on where Eve came from and any details about the span of her lifetime, what was going on, and then I build on this information. Publicly, both in dress and deportment, Eve represented her mistress. Her behavior and dress reflected the household of the Speaker of the House of Burgesses. I believe Eve's behavior would also have reflected her choices and not just those made for her. Slaves took pride in dress and, through my portrayals of Eve, I provide alternative ways of looking at slave women.

I present Eve with pride and dignity, not just in mannerism, outlook, and speech but in her ability to understand her situation. My interpretation is about the strength of black women in Williamsburg and how they dealt with the difficulties of their circumstances.

I am motivated by stories of black women. There are amazing stories about black women that do not get the attention they deserve. I can do my part by sharing the story of Eve, doing her justice.

Wright's interpretation places Eve in the larger community as well.

While I try to understand what Eve's life was like serving in the Randolphs' house, I also place her in the African American community. I look at everything around her, at other slaves on the Randolph property, and I look at enslaved people of other white families. I connect Eve's story with the stories of other enslaved and free women who lived in Williamsburg during the same time period—women like Agnes, who was also with the Randolphs, Lydia Broadnax, who worked at George Wythe's house nearby, as well as Anne Ashby, a free black woman whose husband, Matthew Ashby, was a free black man. I use information about these women to build a picture of the community.

I introduce guests to other characters that we interpret, linking them in stories to life at the Randolph property and to events in the town. I talk about what was going on in the town that impacted enslaved people, like Governor Dunmore's proclamation of 1775 offering freedom to some slaves and the British occupation of the town in 1781. It's like concentric circles—Williamsburg, Virginia Colony, and other colonies.

History is my favorite subject. Not history as a collection of dates, but about real people. You can be creative without making things up. I like to help people question their views of history.

One cardinal rule of interpretation is the need to refrain from spreading misinformation.

You have to arm yourself with as much information as possible so that you know the history. You have to extend the interpretation to the surroundings and associate the community and the family. You have to work with a network of resources.

Yet, new interpreters should not feel intimidated by veteran interpreters. They should not be discouraged about not knowing enough. The work to acquire knowledge and to build skills for interpreting is an ongoing process. You have to always seek new and more information, more research, and more opportunities to develop more skills. You have to always try to get more training and seek more evaluations about your work.

Wright is not afraid to deal with challenging subjects.

Sometimes guests ask questions of a more private nature about Eve or other female characters that I interpret. How do I respond to such questions? It depends on the group. You have to know if it is appropriate to discuss or answer a question at the time or whether you should take particular guests aside to explain things as professionally, factually, and frankly as possible. You have to read the audience; this is important in all cases. While interpreting and presenting your character, you have to be ready to answer any questions about that person. Having a good historical perspective helps me in my performances.

Art Johnson

 ARTHUR JOHNSON has been with Colonial Williamsburg interpreting African American history since the 1980s. He has played characters including Gowan Pamphlet and a slave preacher called Moses, who was a forerunner and associate of Pamphlet. He also interpreted the life of Adam Waterford, a free black cooper. Johnson is currently an actor-interpreter who plays a number of historic African American individuals in Colonial Williamsburg's Revolutionary City programming.

Johnson is a well-known professional storyteller. His storytelling skills come in especially handy when working with children and families and larger groups. Johnson's storytelling is an integral part of some evening programs and educational outreach activities. He also performs at storytelling festivals and community events where he matches stories to occasions. Stories, riddles, and mental puzzles are

especially relevant to Johnson's interpretation of
how slaves used their wit and wisdom to navigate
daily challenges.

For Johnson, asking questions is as important as providing answers.

I've always liked learning about and talking about black history.
I like talking to students and young folks about it. I like to see them
try to come to terms with how they have thought about history and
how different that information is from what they are now learning. It
is important to teach young folks about history. If you don't know what
happened in the past, you are doomed to repeat its mistakes somewhere
in the future. I always ask myself, "Where can I start off with the young
folks?" I ask them if they ever hear about slavery on TV or read about it
on the Internet because the media is their world.

Each audience is different; each one is unique. When I start off with
questions, the answers help me to know how people really think, and
then I can go on from there. Over the years, I have learned to be more
questioning before I start giving answers or trying to get my audience to
derive the answers.

You have to give them the information in the language of the period,
and you do not talk down to anyone. No! Not at all. If you simplify the

interpretation too much, it will lose its power. Folks will respond to you, and they will ask you simple questions. I want questions that will tell me that they understand that slavery is a difficult subject. Because, if I have inspired them, hopefully they will have more questions, and then I can direct them to some books that support my interpretation. I would like to have them walk away thinking about what I have been telling them.

How do I know that my interpretation is making a difference? You get responses that let you know how you are doing. Sometimes people will tell you right there, "I never thought about that or looked at it like this," or they will send letters saying, "It was a great tour. My child loved it. He is doing a report in school about this." You get feedback that lets you know that you have affected that person.

Some questions can be answered only by changing the perspective of the person who asked them. For Johnson, a key to good interpretation is provoking his audience to think differently.

Sometimes when I am presenting a slave character, someone will ask me, "Is your master a good master?" There is no definition of what is a good master. If he is so good a master, would he still own you? He can't be but so good a master if he still owns you. Some masters looked at their slaves as family, so you had that within the relationship. But people have to get a grasp of the fact that a slave is a person who is owned.

One way to teach about the past is to start with something in the present, something familiar.

I've found that you have to relate to your audience before you can get them to relate to you and what you are saying to them. For example, I talk about the buildings in the town. Even when I am not out on

the street, I still talk about the buildings. I want them to look at the town and think about who would be doing the work in these buildings in the eighteenth century. Then I can move on from there and talk about slaves and free blacks in Williamsburg. For them to get to what they don't know, they have to be holding onto something that they do know. I am not trying to grade them or to get deep with them into the subject of African American history, but I do want them to walk away with some knowledge and a basic concept.

What if you have only five minutes with the guests? Five minutes, three hundred seconds. What do you want them to know? Within those three hundred seconds, you have to get them to feel comfortable with you. You have to make them feel that they can ask you a question. You have to make them feel like this guy is worthy of listening to.

I used to train interpreters for "The Other Half Tour," which provided guests with a good overview of slavery and African American life in eighteenth-century Williamsburg. The tour was only supposed to be one hour, but some interpreters took it over this time. They made it as long as ninety minutes. You would be amazed how people stay with you if you are presenting something to them that they want to know about in detail.

Some things are learned the hard way.

I remember doing "The Other Half Tour" and talking about how slaves were like family members to their slave owners. They were family, but they were also property. If their owners got into financial trouble, they would sell them. Then, my audience would say, "It's your family. How could you do that?" I would ask, "How many of you have dogs or other pets? How many of you treat your dogs like they are members of the family? You make sure their health is good, that they have good food, and you travel with them." Then I asked the folks on the tour, "If somebody would come up and say, 'I will give you two million dollars for your dog,' would you sell it?" Typically, the man would say "yes," and the wife would go "no, no!" So a family member that you declared to twenty-some people became property when it came to making money. When I used that same example with a young girl, I said to her, "Would you sell it for two million dollars?" She said, "No!" and started crying. This taught me that this is a very mature subject. I cannot use it as a teaching tool in the same way for children. You learn from doing things.

Johnson uses riddles as well as stories to make his points and get the audience involved and to get them to interact with interpreters.

It is called "edutainment." First, I grab their attention with a riddle. Now I can talk to them. I tell them that, when you are out here on the streets of town, there is no electricity, there is no instant music, and any time you want to do something to have fun, you must create it yourself. One thing that people did back then was create a lot of riddles. I use riddles to get my listeners' attention before I start to talk to them about the history.

One riddle that really has them guessing for a long time is about people in a boat. Here's how it goes: One knight, a man, and his son get into a boat. They row across the river. When they get to the other side, three people get out of the boat. How's that possible?

The thing is that, if you are reading this riddle rather than hearing it, you immediately see the "k" in "knight." But, in telling it orally, "k-n-i-g-h-t" sounds like "n-i-g-h-t." This riddle tests listening and thinking skills. Everyone thinks someone else was rowing the boat, or someone was already in the boat, and some people even suggest that they picked up someone along the way. Lots of times they don't solve it.

Find your passion, and get good at it. Storytelling is an art, not merely a practice that you imitate.

As an interpreter working in a large living history museum, I do different roles and portray different slaves and free blacks. I fill in for different folks at different times. As I told one of our new interpreters, "Do as much as you can to include both day and evening work. If you don't try it out, you won't know it. Once you have done everything, sit down and think about what it is that you really want to do, and go on from there."

I love storytelling, and I also like role playing, but I also enjoy giving information in a lecture format, like a teacher in a classroom, since speaking in my own twenty-first-century voice lets me talk about both the past and present-day society. It helps me know whether or not people understand. But, I think I like storytelling first.

At first, I listened to interpreters who were storytellers, and I knew I wanted to do storytelling. But hearing someone say something and trying to say it as you heard it is not easy. You end up not saying it like you heard it. You have to learn to listen for what you don't hear when you try to tell the same story. And you have to develop your own style.

When someone else tells the same story, the effect is not the same.

My style: I put my whole body into it. I use different voices to represent different characters in the story. Different parts of the story can be manipulated without losing the main message. I often change parts of the story to suit different occasions, and I tell the story to fit the audience.

When you are telling your story, within a minute or two you've got to develop a relationship with your audience. To do this, you say something like, "Good day to you," "How was your day today?" or "Are you having a good day?" You have to know, right away, if they are with you because you are talking to a group of folks that don't have to listen to you. Even when you have a captive audience, it still doesn't mean they have to pay attention.

Now, if you want someone to remember something in your story, you have to repeat it three times. This is an effective way to get someone to remember. A good history teacher is someone who can bring the story alive. The difference between reading and telling is that you can give a better impression of it in telling it. You can explain to someone how to look at and how to see things.

The average historian would not do well here. You can be a historian of eighteenth-century America anywhere, but can you come here and talk to people like the ones with whom I talk to in my interpretation? Historians want to tell you everything, and the average person's mind is not ready to soak up everything. Interpreters and storytellers will introduce something. If people stop, they want to hear it, and if they move on, they don't want to hear it.

The nature of slavery differed depending on the time and place.

Many times people don't know, when you say "slave," what exactly that means. They think of nineteenth-century slavery, and they don't realize that there is a whole history of slavery prior to that time.

When you start talking about slavery in Africa, you are talking about a different kind of slavery that existed over there. So, I start by trying to find out what they know about Africa. I say, "Everybody put your right hand up." Then I say, "Everybody that believes that Africa is a country, keep your right hand up." And those that keep their right hand up let me know that they have no idea. I let them put their hands down.

Then I say, "Everybody put your left hand up," and I say, "All those who believe that Africa is a continent keep your left hand up." And then they would say, "Yeah! That's it, that's it." From there I can start talking about the different countries in Africa that were involved in the slave trade. I am trying to get them to understand slavery in Africa versus slavery in America.

Johnson wants guests to see slavery as more than laws and rules.

I try to get them to understand the personal nature of slavery, and I introduce them to actual people who lived in the past, like Thomas Jefferson's personal manservant Jupiter or George Washington's man

Billy Lee or Peyton Randolph's Johnny or London Carter's slave Nassau, all eighteenth-century Virginians. I give the big picture and then the microscopic image, where I can talk about these individuals. A man who had a slave that he was calling his personal manservant, if they were in the house and there was no one else to talk to, who did he talk to? And you don't think that over a span of ten or twelve years they wouldn't have developed a relationship?

A challenge is when, where, and how to integrate African American history.

My concentration is on African American history, but there are other interpreters here whose concentration is on Native American history or another area in American history. When possible, every site should be discussing all these factors as they relate to whatever is the site's main priority. African Americans played a very important role in the building of the city and in the running of the city, but if you don't hear about it on a regular basis, at the various sites, you may never think that was the case.

Johnson draws from personal history as well as history in general.

I will always have something that the average white person cannot draw upon, and that's my own experience of being black. When I think what slaves had to go through, I can't say that I know exactly what slaves felt but I know what sometimes I feel in this world now. So it is not hard to imagine what it was like when they were in such a demeaning situation, a situation far worse than I will ever have to face. Without a doubt, your ethnicity is bound to affect you.

Rosè McAphee

 ROSEMARIE MCAPHEE has been involved in advancing the goals of African American interpretation at Colonial Williamsburg for almost thirty years. She started as an interpreter in 1985 and today is a training specialist and instructor of interpreters.

Before moving into training and instruction, McAphee worked as a supervisor of interpreters. To some extent, she still serves in that capacity since she observes interpreters in their work and offers feedback. McAphee regularly helps in the planning, executing, and evaluating of a variety of educational programs.

Among her experiences in the field of public history are stage performance, public speaking, storytelling, and singing, which have been useful for on-site programming as well as educational and multimedia outreach. She has portrayed various enslaved and free individuals and presented information as teacher, moderator, and historian. McAphee is also sought by

other historic museums and sites and other organizations to help train interpreters and other staff on
sensitivity and diversity. She has presented at conferences and workshops dealing with living history,
African American history, slavery, and teaching con-
troversial issues.

McAphee stresses the importance of African Americans taking on a range of roles behind the scenes as well as directly working with guests.

Having worked my way up from an entry-level character interpreter to lead interpreter to supervisor to training specialist, I understand how each step prepared me for what I do today. I am grateful for the many people who encouraged me on my journey. Some are no longer here, but they are not forgotten. I feel that I am giving back in that I am helping to teach and inspire others. I draw on my experience to provide leadership and encouragement to both newcomers and veteran interpreters.

It is important for African Americans to be represented in all aspects of historical interpretation and presentation from frontline interpreter to program development to management as well as behind-the-scenes support positions. When we have more African Americans in leading roles, it brings more diversity and more voices to the table. Also, having African Americans in key leadership positions, as Colonial Williamsburg does, inspires more African Americans to want to visit the Historic Area with their families or to apply for the many varied positions available at the organization.

Cultivating the right attitude and aptitude is essential to the practice.

You have to be able to communicate effectively on all levels. Patience is indeed a virtue in this field, and I think I have it in abundance for it is surely needed! When you work for a large well-known organization such as Colonial Williamsburg, sometimes things don't happen quickly, so you must be patient. Humility is important, too, because you have to humble yourself to the history. History is what it is, and sometimes, many times, it isn't pretty, but it is American history, and we need to view it with open eyes.

Mediation skills are very important because, when you present a side of history that challenges the guests' long-held beliefs, you have to be prepared to support and maybe even defend your position. At times, an honest portrayal of the harsher sides of American history can elicit defensiveness or denial from guests. We have to meet them where they are and present our interpretation in such a way as to allow them to see history from a different perspective.

Interpreting—and training interpreters—requires staying up-to-date on the latest research and technology.

I am constantly browsing the new arrival shelves of our John D. Rockefeller, Jr. Library, which has excellent resources for our interpreters and anyone researching eighteenth-century Virginia history.

The basic elements of the job are the same as when I started in 1985, but the technology available to our guests and our staff makes this an exciting and challenging time. We can get information in an instant but must be sure the information is accurate and up-to-date. The foundation is embracing digital technologies and resources, for example, adventures like a combined online and on-site interactive spy game and activities for adults and children on our website.

Over the years, McAphee has seen some real changes in how guests have responded to African American interpretation.

Initially, in the 1980s, guest responses ranged from skepticism, hesitance, and caution to curiosity, excitement, and a thirst for more. This changed as the wider society became more exposed to popular public programming about slavery like television series on the subject. The history-making television event *Roots* that premiered in 1977 not only had an immediate and profound impact but a long-term one as well. The interest in the story of Kunta Kinte, a West African man who was brought as a slave to Maryland in 1767 and sold to a Virginian planter, and his descendants sparked interest in what historians were calling "social history." It was not the history of wars, conquests, empires, etcetera, but it was the stories of everyday people living their lives in a different time and place. That also impacted the types of programs and exhibits that museums began to present.

Our African American program offerings matured in the 1990s and 2000s. A number of factors contributed to this. First was the development of a separate department to focus solely on African American interpretations and programs. The department was founded shortly after I came. This allowed the staff to have creative control over the development and implementation of programs highlighting the African American experience. In the late 1980s, the foundation reconstructed a slave quarter at Carter's Grove plantation at a location identified through archaeological excavations as a site of domestic and farm-related dwellings dating to the eighteenth century. The complex was reconstructed using eighteenth-century tools and techniques by Colonial Williamsburg's Historic Trades carpenters.

From the 1990s to the first years of the 2000s, African American interpretation was in full swing. I should say that other factors contributed to this more receptive climate. For example, there was a series of conferences about interpretation of slavery at places like museums and historic sites that was presented at several key sites, such as here and Monticello, where newly energized staff were expanding the interpretation of the enslaved workers. As guests began to see this type of interpretation at a number of historic houses and sites, they were not as shocked to come upon an inclusive presentation and actually began to seek out the experience.

Interacting with guests can be frustrating . . . or rewarding.

One time, at the Benjamin Powell House with Emily James, we had
just completed our interpretation to a group of adult guests when one
of the ladies stayed back. She was from another country. After all the
other guests had left, she came over to us with a most serious look on
her face and said in a soft voice, "Ladies, my husband has gone to get
our car. He's going to pull up to that gate over there and we are going
to free you! I can't believe that they still hold slaves in America!" We
came to the conclusion that we had done our job so well—along with
our fellow white interpreters Kristen Spivey and the late John Lowe—
that she really believed we were slaves! Emily and I sat on each side of

her, put our arms around her, and assured her that we were not really slaves and would be going home to our families at five o'clock.

Another time I was at the Thomas Everard House giving a tour, and at the end an elderly African American lady approached me. As she shook my hand to thank me for the tour, she slipped some money into it. I said, "Oh, thank you so much, ma'am, but we can't accept tips. I'm only doing my job, so the fact that you were moved by it is enough for me." She said, "No, I want you to have it to get yourself a cold drink or something." I again said, "No, ma'am, we can't accept tips." She took my hand into hers and looked me in the eye with all tenderness and sweetness and said, "Well, do they search you, baby?" We both broke out into a fit of giggles, and I said, "No, ma'am, thank you so very much!"

An interpreter has to gauge when to change and when to hold firm.

I was giving "The Other Half Tour" and came to the section about comparing the Church of England to the Baptist church during the Great Awakening. I described the Church of England as "boring." Well, I had two ladies who were Anglican, and they politely came up after the tour to question me about my impression. Since then I use the phrase "organized and structured" instead of "boring."

Another time, when I was a supervisor, another supervisor approached me and said, "You know, I've always felt that our slave characters were just too clean. I mean, if they were working all day, they would be dirty, right? That would make it more realistic." I said, "As soon as you identify some white working-class character to also 'dirty up,' we can talk." I explained to the supervisor that, if we only have the enslaved characters dirty, then we will reinforce the misconception that slaves (and therefore black people in general) were dirty and slovenly. This was also the capital city of one of the largest and richest colonies, so the enslaved here were probably *not* all dirty since they represented their masters when they were out and about the city. It was never mentioned again.

Our main goal is identified in the foundation's motto, "That the future may *learn* from the past." It is not necessary to re-create *every* nuance of the past in order to learn valuable lessons for the present and future. In fact, some things from the past should *stay* in the past! We don't always have to relive it to better understand it or to teach it.

Creating African American characters can be particularly taxing.

We are far more challenged to find historical documentation about African Americans, women, the middling, and poor people than for prominent whites who lived in Williamsburg or visited there frequently during the eighteenth century. The vast majority of these lesser-known individuals could neither read nor write and therefore left behind few if any documents, the most fundamental source for historians. The details of their lives were often not deemed worthy to be written down or are written from the perspective of the dominant culture, such as in parish registers and county court records like wills and inventories, criminal cases, and deeds of manumission. Even so, these records, if used carefully, can provide key dates for enslaved and free blacks. However, many eighteenth-century county records in Virginia were burned during the Civil War making it difficult to find more information about everyday life.

We still struggle in determining what "appropriate documentation" is for presenting slavery, especially because of this overall dearth of information from the perspectives of enslaved people. Even working with the available records leaves many gaps, a problem also, though not as extreme, for interpreters who portray well-documented historical figures such as George Washington, Thomas Jefferson, and Patrick Henry. Interpreters still have to use some historic license to fill in the details of people's lives—particularly their personal or private lives—in order to present an individual as a "complete" person of the past.

There are ways to surmount these hurdles and establish legitimacy.

We have to include a diverse assortment of historical voices. We have to look for evidence beyond the documents. For example, if we are using a letter written by an eighteenth-century Williamsburg resident, we look for other evidence, preferably created by someone other than the letter writer, to support what it says. We often use the knowledge gained from archaeological evidence and from the works of cultural anthropologists and social historians to provide context for the documents, to provide wider perspectives, and to fill in the gaps about life in the past. Although written documentation is an essential source, interpretation cannot be based solely on it because we know that written evidence, even official records, are not necessarily objective. Also, if we limit interpretation only to what is specifically documented for any given person, we go back to telling very little about the lives of most eighteenth-century Virginians.

Interpreting is more than re-creating and presenting a comprehensive picture of the past.

An interpreter has to have an interest in lifelong learning. We are continually researching and discovering new things as well as revising interpretations, programs, sites as needed. An interpreter has to be open-minded—able to accept information that may challenge his or her long-held beliefs. These are the things that I say to new interpreters.

I also tell them that it is important that they come with the desire to interact with people. If you don't like interacting with people, this isn't the job for you.

Are new interpreters easier to teach than veteran ones?

Each group has its own unique rewards and challenges. New hires are wide-eyed and ready to go. We have to focus and direct that energy in the right way so that they are successful and the guests receive excellent guest service. Veterans already know quite a bit, and most of them continually research in areas of interest. We sometimes have to challenge their concept of "I already know all this" or "I like the way we *used* to do things." We try to encourage them to be open to new ideas, information, and concepts. We also appreciate their frontline experience

and can engage them as mentors or peer leaders for their coworkers.

I'm constantly inspired by the interpreters, guests, and visiting scholars who are committed to telling an inclusive story, especially our new hires. I am always open to learning, and both new hires and veteran interpreters help to keep me focused. In some ways, they help me keep abreast of new scholarship as they pose new questions that allow me to refine my approaches and continually update my ways of seeing and doing things. Interpreting and training create not only an engaging learning environment but a place where the facilitators themselves can also learn.

Greg James

 GREGORY JAMES was best known for his signature character, a slave called Wil. Wil is based on a specific, documented person named Will who was a slave at the Raleigh Tavern and probably helped with the horses. James liked to say playfully that Wil is spelled with one *W,* one *i,* and one *l,* making it "Wil." It was his way of individualizing Wil's story and making it memorable to guests. He used tools like files, hammers, nails, and horseshoes from a special toolbox he carried to enliven his presentations.

Many guests recall their encounters with Wil as their most memorable Colonial Williamsburg experiences. He uplifted their spirits and increased their understanding of the everyday life of a slave in eighteenth-century Williamsburg. James was also famous for his singing: his voice vibrated through the streets of the Historic Area. He would invite others, much to their surprise, to join him in a call-and-response style of singing, and they would happily do so. Greg James died on April 23, 2013.

Singing was just one of the hooks James used to connect with guests.

You have to some way or another connect to the individual. You have to find several hooks, hoping that the individual will take a hold onto one of the hooks. Once you get them with that hook, then you can pitch it to them, then you can teach them, particularly some African Americans, who don't wish to hear the story about slavery.

Many people like to forget about that part of history so as not to be reminded of the brutality and the injustice. They don't want to be reminded of people beaten, lashed, and currycombed [a currycomb is

Will

Will was an enslaved man in the household of Anthony Hay when Hay died in late 1770. He appeared in Hay's estate inventory valued at £60. In a notice in a January 17, 1771, *Virginia Gazette*, the executors of Hay's estate announced that the Raleigh Tavern was to be sold on March 6. The same notice advertised another event, on May 7, a sale that included "nineteen NEGROES belonging to the said Estate, among them a very good Cabinet Maker, a good Coachman and Carter, some fine Waiting Boys, good Cooks, Washers, &c." James Southall purchased the Raleigh Tavern and Will. Southall paid £101 for Will, and for the years of 1783, 1784, and 1786, he was recorded in the Williamsburg personal property tax listings as living in Southall's household.

an instrument with iron points used to comb a horse] or even with one of the limbs of the body being chopped off. But would history be true without it? And when you bring out the fact that blacks fought in the Revolutionary War and that those enslaved African Americans who fought in the American Revolutionary War were given freedom and land at the end of the war, about $3.65 a month as a pension, not many people know about that. Not many people, black or white.

Anthony Hay's estate inventory

Viriginia Gazette notice

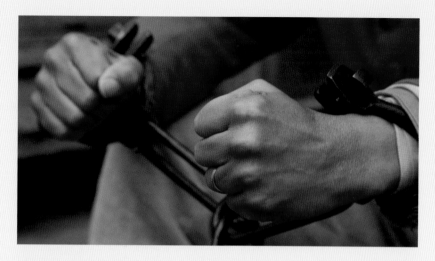

African American audiences often don't like the idea of seeing people portraying slaves.

It can be extremely difficult. One of my hardest hurdles was to interpret to African American audiences. They would look at you; they would roll their eyes at you. But within my twenty-five years of being here with Colonial Williamsburg, I have grown tremendously. I learned to relate to our guests, to connect to them, and once I do those things, I can educate them. I teach history in an elementary manner but not so elementary that it will insult the intelligence of an adult.

It reminds me of a lady who used to live across the street from my grandmother. She said to me, "Greg, what do you do at Colonial Williamsburg?" I said, "Well, I am an interpreter." She said, "Well, what do you interpret?" I said, "Well, I portray a character." So she said, "What character do you portray?" I said, "Well, I portray a slave." "Greg, I don't know how you do that. I don't want any part of that." I said, "What do you mean?" "Greg, I don't need to be reminded of where we come from and how we were beaten and the injustice and so on and so forth." I said, "I tell you what, why don't you come to one of the programs and see for yourself and you can judge for yourself."

It took her awhile, but she finally came to one. The program was called "Remember Me." Later on in the week, she called me up, and she said, "Wow!" That was her first word, even before she said "good morning." "That was incredible!" she said. "Greg, I had no idea that was part of the history." There is an African proverb: Not to know is bad; not to wish to know is worse.

Whites, too, have a range of reactions to the story of slavery.

I don't want to use the word "confused," but a lot of them don't know what to make of it. Some of them nod their heads as though, "yeah, that's history," while others have come to me sobbing and apologized, apologized to me. They didn't do anything to *me!* "I am so sorry," they tell me, "so sorry for what we did to you people."

I remember when I portrayed an African along with James Ingram, who portrays Gowan Pamphlet, in the program "Thy Rod and Thy Staff." I was portraying this African who was used to his custom, his way of religion, not Christianity. Gowan wanted his blessing, but one time the character that I portrayed wasn't going to give Gowan Pamphlet his blessing. He figured that this is the white man's religion. To make a long story short, after the program I went about twenty or twenty-five yards on the street and sat on some steps, just meditating, still in character. And this little old man, God bless his heart, he could hardly walk, was walking with his walking stick, and he looked around to the left and he looked around to his right. Maybe he didn't want anybody to see him, but he came up to me and he said, "I am sorry that my grandfather did that to you. I am sorry." He was sobbing and it touched me, touched me tremendously. That's when I know I am reaching out and connecting with that person.

If you don't like to deal with people, this is not the job for you. Period! I don't know of a better way of saying it: if you don't like to deal with children, crying babies, elderly, whites, prejudiced people, this is not the place for you. If you handle yourself in a professional way when individuals say prejudiced things to you, they will make themselves look foolish. During my first year here, a man asked me, "Look here, where can I get my shoes shined? You shine shoes?" I kept my composure. "No, sir. You go down to Merchants Square and they might shine your shoes for you, if you have the right amount of money, but we don't do that here." And then I looked at him with a slight smile but with a look, and I tell you, he was quite embarrassed.

Portraying a slave in scenes involving a white character in authority can be challenging.

You have to have communication. You have to have that relationship with your peers, black and white, but specifically with the white individuals who portray a sheriff, a slave patrol, or a constable. If you have a good relationship, a natural relationship, you can relate very well. You know where that fine line is, and I encourage the other interpreter to do his job. If he wants to pretend that he is grabbing me, I tell him, "Go ahead, go ahead. You alright with me, man." You see, we have that relationship. I like keeping it real, so I want him to internalize and to be true to history. Otherwise you would be putting on something that . . . it wouldn't be true history. The guests need to see this strong programming, for it makes my job easier to reach out to them. It will provoke their minds.

Interpreting requires all sorts of preparation, and not just during work hours.

You have to keep up with your training in history. The Colonial Williamsburg Foundation offers several types of training, like diversity, sensitivity, and communication training. You are trained on how to deal with disabled persons, like people in wheelchairs. I use all of the training to my advantage.

I really have to spiritually prepare myself and mentally prepare myself to reach an audience. I have to be spiritually prepared for the day, from the moment when I wake up to the time I step foot on Colonial Williamsburg's property. That's how I do it. And thank God for that because He has equipped me to be able to handle situations like "shine my shoes" and other challenges. And, yes, even if it takes a song or two, I will meditate in my heart to prepare for the day. When I leave work, it takes me a good hour to unwind, a good hour to relax and realize—Greg, Greg, knock, knock!—you are back to the present.

I do carry it home with me. I think about that difference that I made in that child that day, that difference I made in that adult, that difference that I made in that young teenager who is struggling through adolescence, that difference I made in that teenage boy who cannot make his decision on what he wants to do with his life, that difference that I made in that elderly husband who had just lost his wife. My mission is Colonial Williamsburg's motto, "That the future may learn from the past." Yeah, but does the future really learn from the past? Many people don't learn from the past. My mission is, until the day I die, until the day I leave Colonial Williamsburg, to continue to make that difference to the littlest child.

I like folks to remember that a lot of this bickering, both among blacks and whites, a lot of this doing people wrong or doing your fellow men wrong, being rude to them and cruel to them—if they would truly learn from the past, they would know how to treat their fellow man. That would truly make a difference.

When I present a character, I like to make it as real as possible, and to me, to a certain extent, that's not acting. That's the difference between an actor and a character. This is history. You are talking about real people. That's what makes it a little different. You are not talking about any John Doe or Jane Doe or any cartoon characters.

Working with children came easily for James.

I have seen and I have interpreted to children as young as three and four years old, and they came back when they were seven and eight and remembered me. They come back now that they are in college and still remember me.

If you can make kids happy, you will make their parents happy. I remember, not too long ago, I had several children who, while they were in middle school, didn't like history. One parent told me, "Greg, you're not going to believe this. Remember our child who said she didn't like history? Guess what she is majoring in? She wants to be a history teacher." That made my day.

A lot of this comes natural to me. I know of parents who brought their children from Colorado, Ohio, Georgia, and Florida. They particularly came here looking for Wil. That's beautiful, and you have the child saying, "Mammy, Mammy, let's go to Colonial Williamsburg, let's go to Colonial Williamsburg. I want to see Wil, I want to see Wil."

I walk around with a toolbox full of horseshoes and hammers. Children like hands-on presentations. Children like to dance, children like to sing. So with the tools, you show them, even little four year olds. You show them a horseshoe and ask, "You know what this is?" And then they start thinking. I give them a hint. I say, "Could I put this on a cow?" and then they say, "No." Then I say, "Do you put that on a duck—quack, quack!" Then they start laughing. I got them going. These are hooks that I throw out even to a four-year-old child. They shake their head, and then I say, "Should I put it on a horse?" Then they nod their head and look at their mother and dad, and then they say, "That's right, that's right, horse!" And then I say, "That's right, but does the horse go 'moo, moo'?" And they start laughing, and finally I got them to talk. My point is you come down to a child's level. You have to find the tools to use to reach out to that four- or five-year-old child. Children can tell when you are genuine, when you are real. They can feel it.

Everyone has a gift even if he or she might not have tapped into it as yet. Everyone! Many people can't do what I do. I can't do a lot of things other people can do. It's like having a body, head, eyes, nose, mouth, ears, toes, fingers, hands, knees, feet: all of our gifts are part of that body. No gift is more important than the other. The fingers, the toes, the hands, the eyes, the mouth, the head all make up that body. Use

your gift to the fullest. Whatever it is, use it to reach out to the littlest child or to the oldest person.

When you do that, everyone benefits. The little child benefits because she gets knowledge and wisdom, and she is growing. Meanwhile, their moms don't have to drag them to come here because they are coming on their own will, and when they get older, they are bringing their children and, later, their grandchildren. That four year old will be bringing *his* grandchildren here.

Afterword

Historical interpretation is a skill and an art, a moment and a process. As evident in these reflections about this practice and craft at Colonial Williamsburg, a good living history interpretation helps people relate to history. Interpretations are infused with the personality of the interpreter as well as that of the historical character. This playful blending of past and present creates a suspension of disbelief that allows the audience to imagine that the character interpreter *is* that someone from the past. Colonial Williamsburg's character interpreters pull guests into the past. Guests can see, hear, and receive answers to their questions. This interactive process makes history come alive.

It is where the past meets, and sometimes even collides with, the present.

I am grateful for the help of many Colonial Williamsburg colleagues with this project. I am especially grateful to the six interpreters who shared their stories, their techniques, and their hopes.

As I interacted with them, I felt surrounded by their sense of playfulness as well as the seriousness with which they confront the challenges of interpreting sensitive issues. Their work is defined and even hemmed in by historical scholarship, but they are driven by sound judgment and by the need to explore possibilities. They avoid canned interpretation. They interpret slavery with knowledge, fortitude, and forbearance and provide important lessons for practitioners, observers, and others interested in the past and in the field of historical interpretation, especially African American interpretation. In a nutshell, they capture the art and soul of interpreting.

SOURCES FOR HISTORICAL IMAGES

15 Gowan Pamphlet's deed of manumission, York County, Va., Court Records, Deed Book 7 (1791–1809), p. 92, Yorktown, Va. John D. Rockefeller, Jr. Library, Colonial Williamsburg Foundation (CWF) microfilm M-1.18.

17 *Minutes of the Baptist Dover Association, Held at Hickory-Neck Meeting-House, James City County, Virginia. October 12th, 1799* (Richmond, 1799), p. 3. Courtesy, American Antiquarian Society. Early American Imprints microform, series 1, no. 35420 © 2002 by the American Antiquarian Society and NewsBank Inc.

35 Eighteenth-century law about the status of children in Virginia, from William Waller Hening, *The Statutes at Large; Being a Collection of All the Laws of Virginia, from the First Session of the Legislature, in the Year 1619*, vol. 2 (New York, 1823), 170.

37 Record of Cumbo's lawsuit against Adam White, York County, Va., Court Records, Order Book 1774–1784, p. 162, Yorktown, Va. CWF microfilm M-1.33.

47 "Inventory and Appraisement of the Estate of Peyton Randolph Esq. in York County taken Jany. the 5th 1776," York County, Va., Court Records, Wills and Inventories, Book 22 (1771–1783), p. 341, Yorktown, Va. CWF microfilm M-1.11.

47 Bruton Parish Register, 1662–1797, July 6, 1766, p. 37, Bruton Parish Church, Williamsburg. CWF microfilm M-120.

48 *Virginia Gazette, or, the American Advertiser* (Richmond), Feb. 9, 1782. CWF microfilm M-1024, 1–2.

49 Betty Randolph's will, York County, Va., Court Records, Wills and Inventories, Book 23 (1783–1811), pp. 4–5, Yorktown, Va. CWF microfilm 1.12.

91 "Inventory and Appraisement of the Estate of Anthony Hay Late of the City of Williamsburg Tavern Keeper Deceased," Feb. 2, 1771, York County, Va., Court Records, Wills and Inventories, Book 22 (1771–1783), p. 341, Yorktown, Va. CWF microfilm M-1.11.

e and Dixon's *Virginia Gazette* (Williamsburg), Jan. 17, 1771.